BUILDING BLOCKS OF COMPUTER SCIENCE

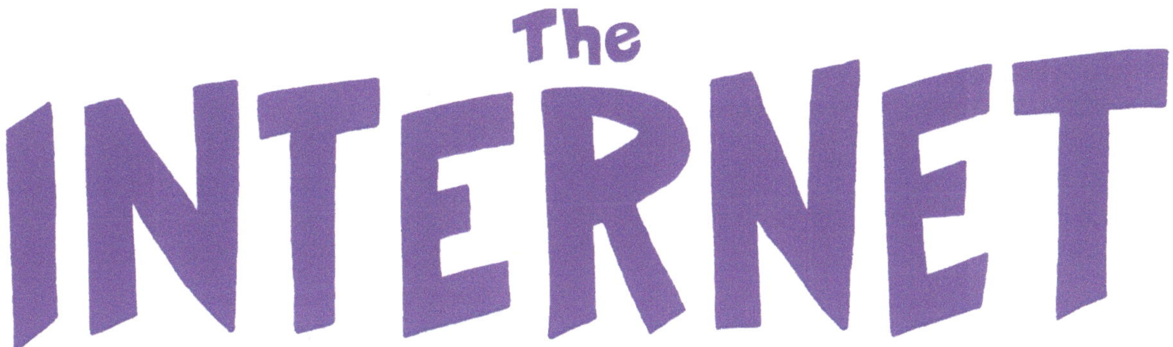

Written by Echo Elise González

Illustrated by Graham Ross

a Scott Fetzer company
Chicago

World Book, Inc.
180 North LaSalle Street
Suite 900
Chicago, Illinois 60601
USA

For information about other World Book publications, visit our website at **www.worldbook.com** or call **1-800-WORLDBK (967-5325).**
For information about sales to schools and libraries, call 1-800-975-3250 (United States), or 1-800-837-5365 (Canada).

Library of Congress Cataloging-in-Publication Data for this volume has been applied for.

Building Blocks of Computer Science
ISBN: 978-0-7166-2883-5 (set, hc.)

The Internet
ISBN: 978-0-7166-3388-4

Also available as:
ISBN: 978-0-7166-2899-6 (e-book)

1st printing August 2020

STAFF

Executive Committee
President: Geoff Broderick
Vice President, Finance: Donald D. Keller
Vice President, Marketing: Jean Lin
Vice President, International Sales: Maksim Rutenberg
Vice President, Technology: Jason Dole
Director, Editorial: Tom Evans
Director, Human Resources: Bev Ecker

Editorial
Manager, New Content: Jeff De La Rosa
Writer: Echo Elise González
Proofreader: Nathalie Strassheim

Digital
Director, Digital Product Development: Erika Meller
Digital Product Manager: Jon Wills

Graphics and Design
Sr. Visual Communications Designer: Melanie Bender
Coordinator, Design Development and Production: Brenda B. Tropinski
Sr. Web Designer/Digital Media Developer: Matt Carrington

Acknowledgments:
Art by Graham Ross/The Bright Agency
Series reviewed by Peter Jang/Actualize Coding Bootcamp

TABLE OF CONTENTS

There is a glossary on page 30. Terms defined in the glossary are in type **that looks like this** on their first appearance.

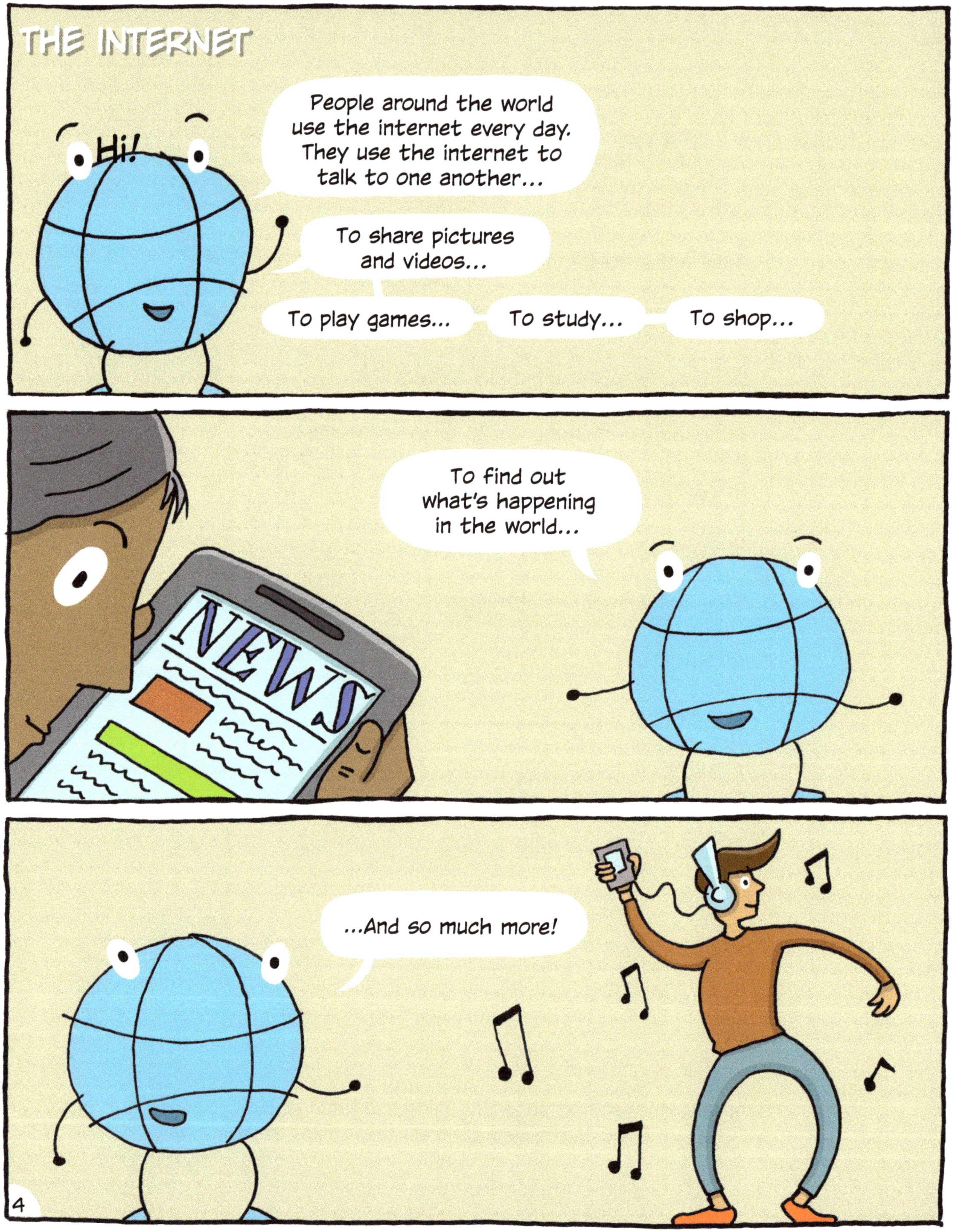

THE INTERNET

Hi!

People around the world use the internet every day. They use the internet to talk to one another...

To share pictures and videos...

To play games...

To study...

To shop...

NEWS

To find out what's happening in the world...

NEWS
People use the internet so much that it may be hard for you to imagine what life was like before it was invented.
But, how often do we stop to think about what the internet is... and how it works?
I'm here to help you understand how the internet works.
INTERNET
I'm the **World Wide Web.** But you can just call me Web.
I'm a part of the internet!

COMPUTER NETWORKS
Some computers work just fine on their own.
But, it's often helpful for multiple computers to be connected.
The connections help computers to share certain resources, such as access to a printer.
WHIRR
The connections help computers to communicate information to one another, too.
A group of connected computers form a **computer network.**
There are different kinds of computer networks.
NETWORK

A local-area network (LAN) connects computers in a single location, such as an office or a school.

A wide-area network (WAN) can connect computers over a large area. It can even connect computers in different countries.

The internet is a WAN. The internet is the world's largest network.
It connects computers and computer networks around the world!

The Internet even includes computers in outer space!

THE HARDWARE OF THE INTERNET
The internet is a giant network made up of smaller **computer networks.**
It links billions of computers and devices.
The internet enables these computers to share **data** with one another. Data is information.
DATA
Computers use and share data in the form of electrical signals.

The data is shared over a wide variety of **hardware.**

Every computer, smartphone, tablet, and any other device that can connect to the internet is part of the internet's hardware.

Telephone lines and cables carry the electronic signals from one computer or network to the next.

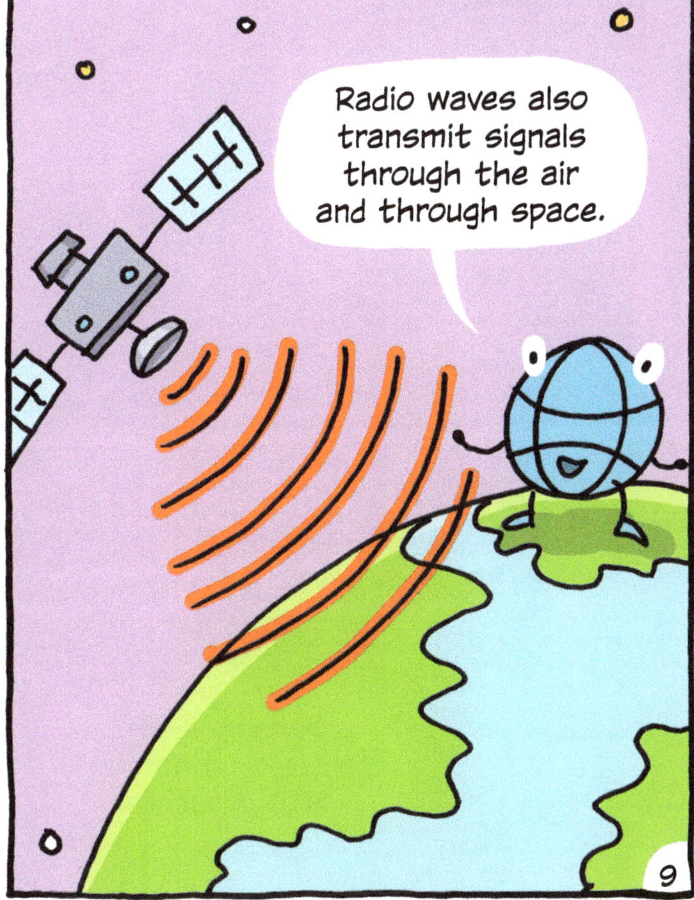
Radio waves also transmit signals through the air and through space.

Computers and devices can access the internet by connecting to the cables that carry the electrical signals...
...or by sending and receiving radio waves.
Internet connections made through the use of radio waves are called wireless connections.
Servers are a special kind of computer that store **data** for sharing over a network.
Servers can store a lot of data.
Servers share data with a network of computers.

The internet relies on millions of servers.
These servers "serve" data to billions of computers and devices!
A device that requests information from a server over the internet is called a **client.**
A client sends a request for information to the server. The server receives the request, then sends the information back to the client.
meow
That's how you can access words, pictures, and other information on the internet!

HOW DATA MOVES OVER THE INTERNET

192.0.2.251

192.0.2.033

198.51.100.247

Every device that is connected to the internet has an **IP address.**

198.51.100.183

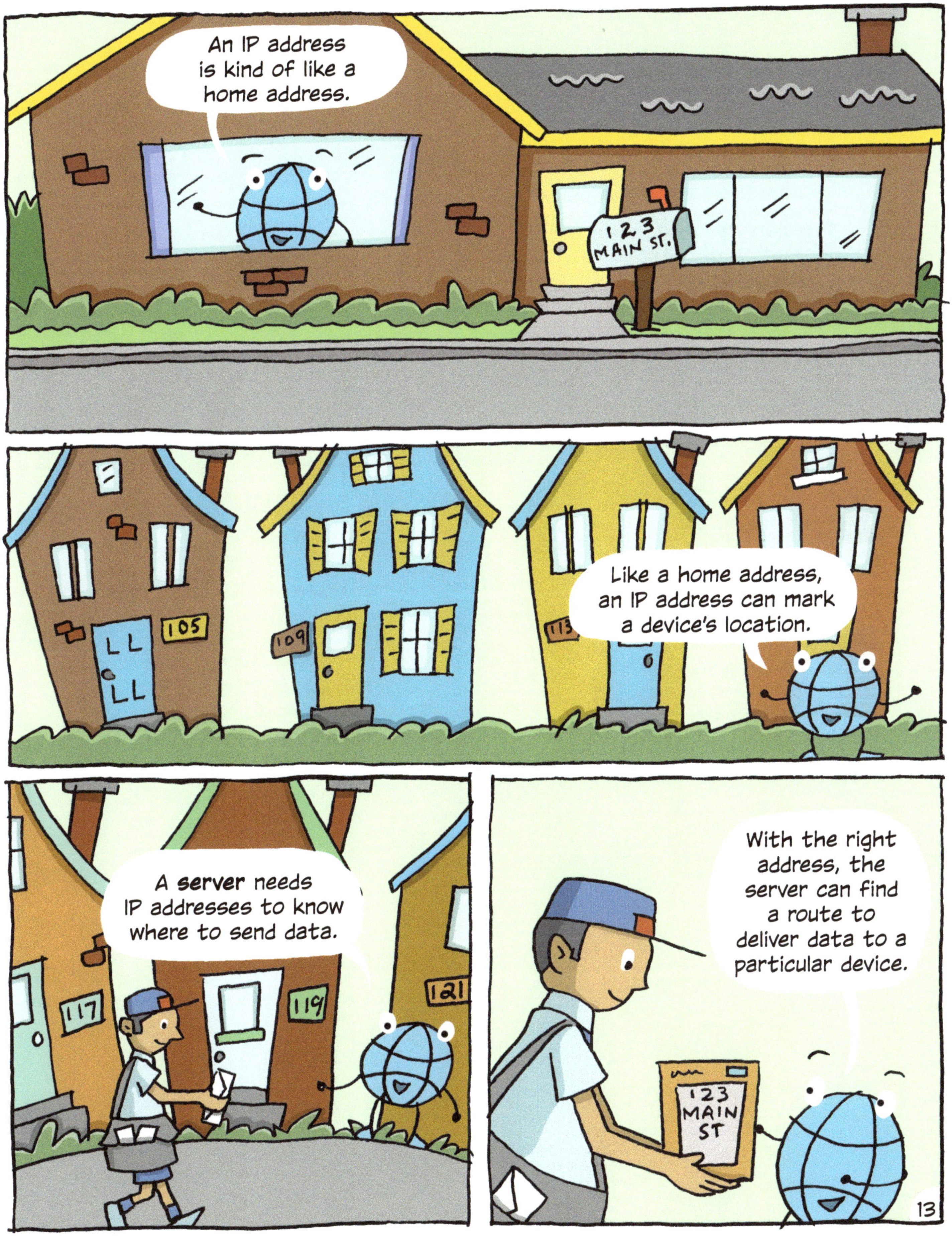

An IP address is kind of like a home address.

Like a home address, an IP address can mark a device's location.

The small chunks are called **packets.** Your phone uses radio signals to send the packets to nearby cell towers.

IP makes use of a trick called **packet switching** to transmit **data.**

Imagine sending a picture from your phone to your computer over the internet.

First, the data making up your picture would be split into small chunks.

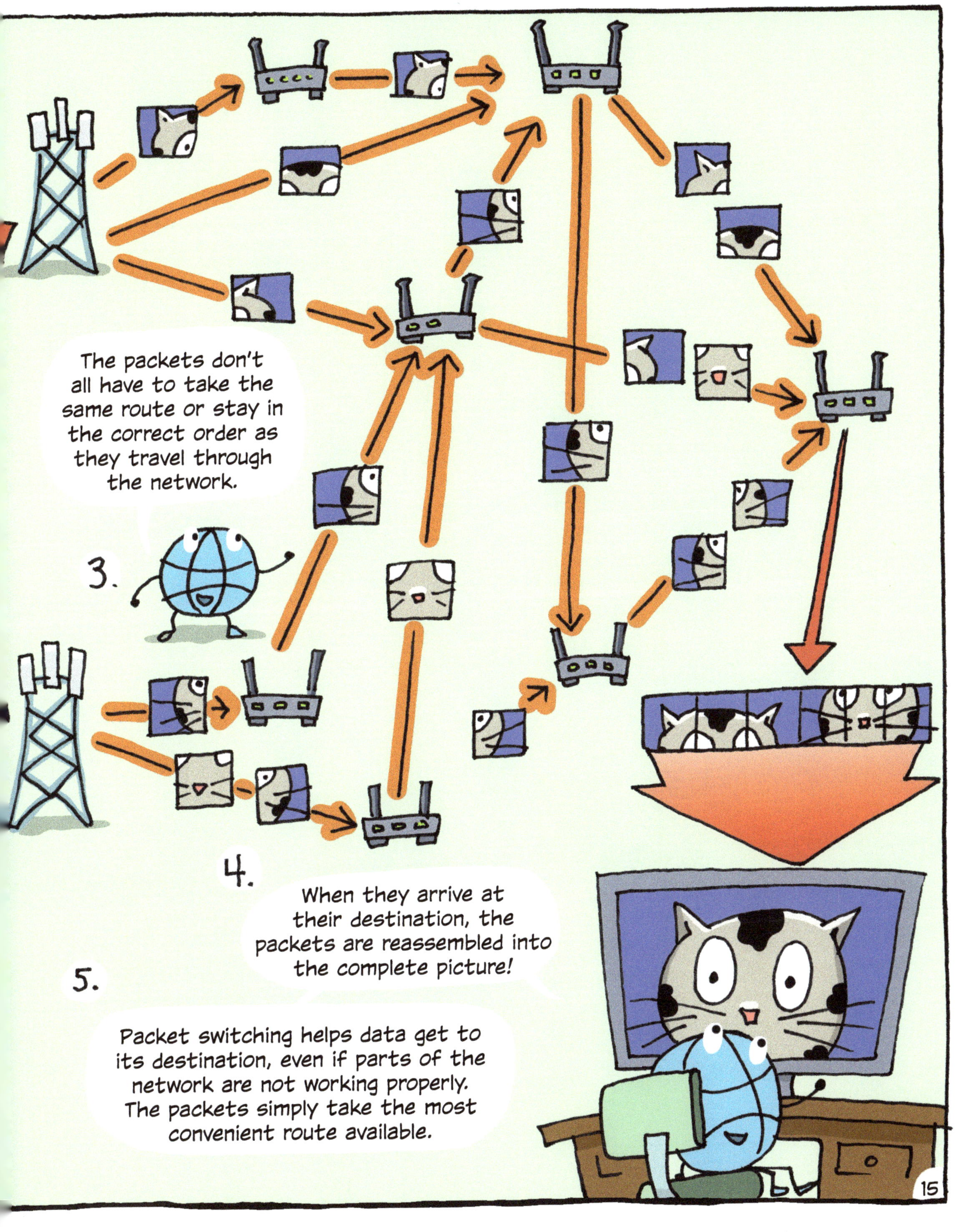
The packets don't all have to take the same route or stay in the correct order as they travel through the network.
3.
4.
When they arrive at their destination, the packets are reassembled into the complete picture!
5.
Packet switching helps data get to its destination, even if parts of the network are not working properly. The packets simply take the most convenient route available.

INTERNET APPLICATIONS

The internet can be used to send emails.

TAP TAP

Hi Web!

Hi Al, it's been too long.

Hi guys!

It can also be used to chat.

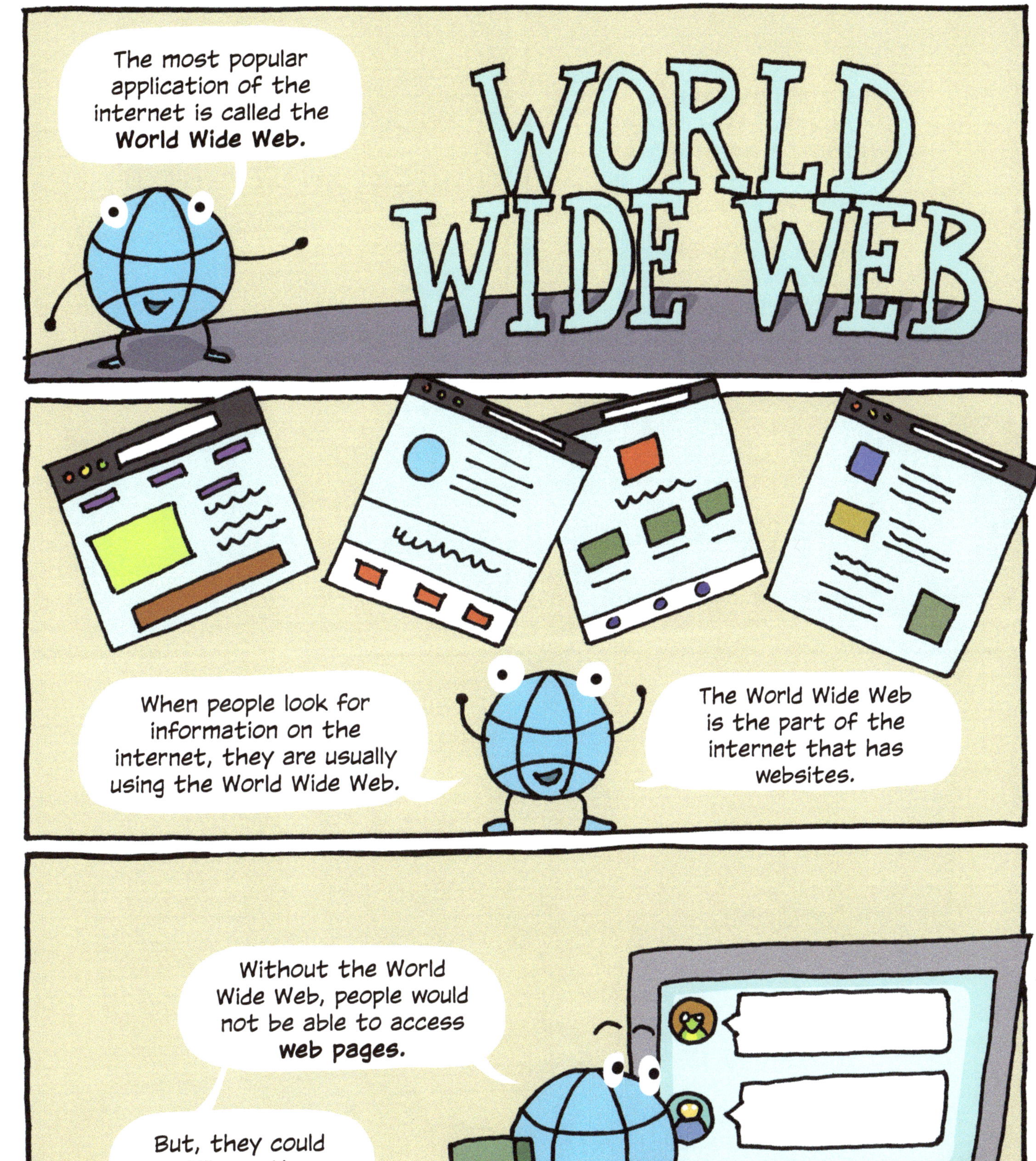
The most popular application of the internet is called the **World Wide Web.**
WORLD WIDE WEB
When people look for information on the internet, they are usually using the World Wide Web.
The World Wide Web is the part of the internet that has websites.
Without the World Wide Web, people would not be able to access **web pages.**
But, they could still use the internet to chat or send emails.

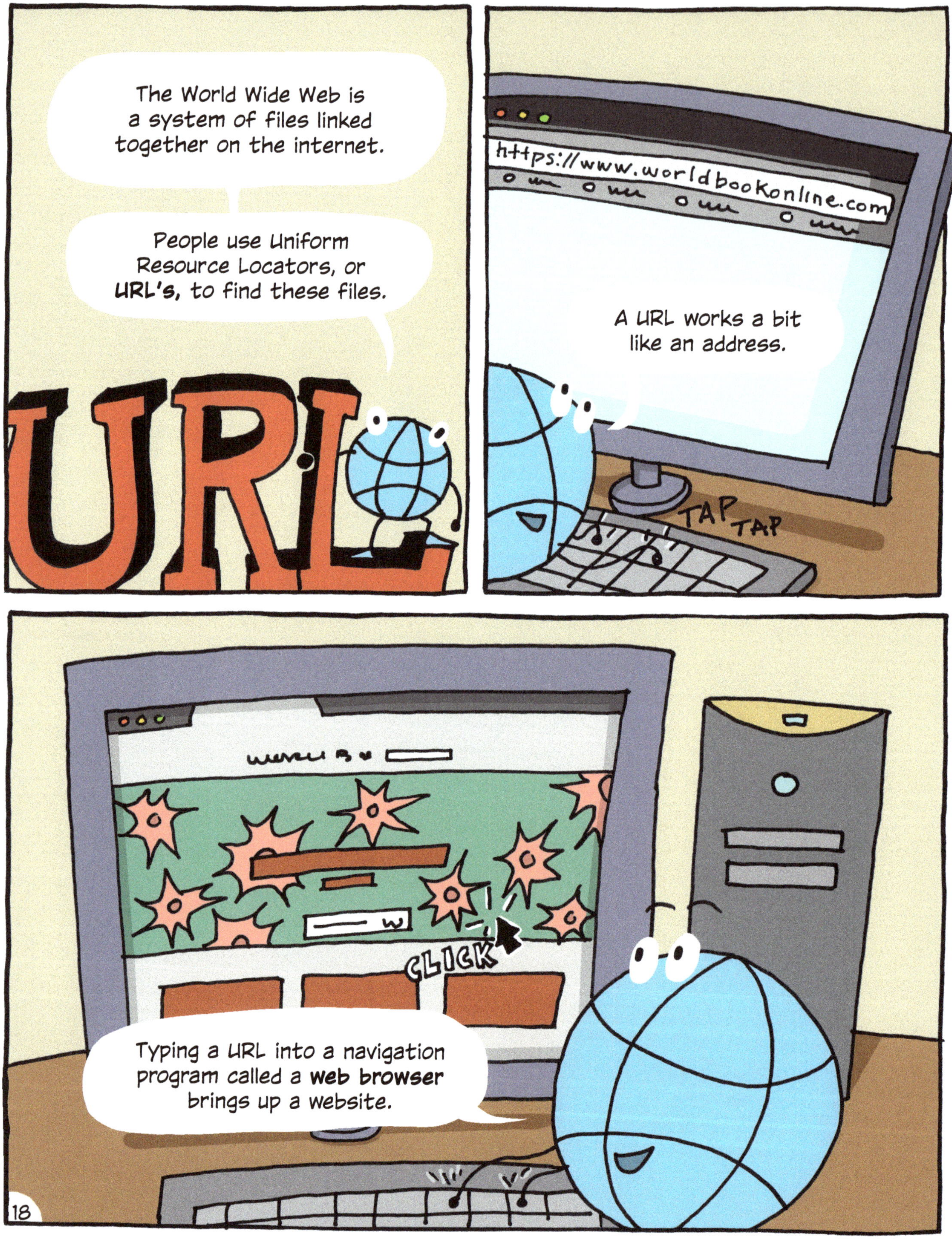

CLICK

Typing a URL into a navigation program called a **web browser** brings up a website.

A website is a location on the World Wide Web containing **web pages** that are linked to each other.
Web pages are digital files.
Goby

People can interact with web pages to find information, listen to music, view images or videos, play games, shop, and more.

Some web pages allow users to transfer **data** from a server to their computer. This is called **downloading.**

Some web pages also allow people to add data to a server. This is called **uploading.**

For many people, the internet is a normal part of daily life.
It's kind of like running water or electric power...
People use it so much that they don't even think about it!

One of the most helpful uses of the internet is file-sharing.
Before the internet, it was more difficult for people to share computer files, especially if they were far away from each other.
Today, the internet makes file-sharing a breeze!
Similarly, the internet helps people communicate with one another quickly.
It gives people more tools for communication.
Hi
Hi!
Hi!

IT'S IN THE CLOUD!
The internet is an important tool for sharing files, communicating, and more.
Another important use for the internet is storing **data.**
When people store and process their data through the internet, instead of just on their own machine, it is called **cloud computing.**
In cloud computing, people like to say that their data is being stored "in the cloud."

But the data is not stored in an actual cloud in the sky.
Although, that would be cool!
1 1 0 1 1 0 0 0 0 1 0 1 0 1

In reality, the data is stored in one or more of the internet's **servers.**

...Which is still pretty cool!

Keeping data in the cloud helps to keep it safe.
SAVE
TAP

BOOM
Data that's stored on multiple servers is less likely to get lost.
If something happens to one of the servers, there are backup copies in other locations.

Storing data in the cloud can also save memory space on your device.
This is especially helpful when storing really big files!
MEMORY

THE INTERNET OF THINGS
Another cool way that people use the internet is to connect everyday objects.
MAKE COFFEE
CLICK
Computers used to be gigantic. Some were the size of a whole room!
Over time, they got smaller...
TAP
And smaller...

Now, lots of information can be stored on a tiny **computer chip!**
HI EVERYBODY

Because computer chips are so small, it's easy to *embed* (place) them in many different kinds of devices, including thermostats, doorbells, and even coffee makers.
Some of these **embedded computers** can connect to the internet.

People call the system of internet-linked objects the **Internet of Things (IoT).**
IOT

Objects that are connected to one another or to a computer or other device over the internet are part of the Internet of Things.
mmmm!

Researchers in the United States began developing the internet during the 1960's and 1970's.

It was originally designed for military purposes.

The designers wanted a way to communicate messages that couldn't be *intercepted* (stopped) by the enemy.

Packet switching could keep messages safe by breaking them up and sending them along different paths. So, if the enemy tried to intercept the message at one spot, they would only catch part of it.

HUH?

In 1990, the British computer scientist Tim Berners-Lee wrote the **software** for the **World Wide Web.**

He wanted to make a "place" where information could be organized and shared.

The invention of personal computers and the **World Wide Web** made it easier for ordinary people to use the internet—not just computer scientists.
During the 2000's and 2010's, internet connections became commonplace.
Internet connections also became faster.
CLICK
SEND

Faster internet connections enabled people to do more over the internet.

The streaming of movies and music became hugely popular. The internet has only been around for a few decades...

...but it has changed so much about how we live.

Imagine how much the internet could change our lives in 100 years!

GLOSSARY

client a computer that requests data from a server over the internet.

cloud computing using internet servers to store and process data.

computer chip a tiny piece of silicon that holds an electronic circuit. A circuit is a loop that an electric current can follow.

computer network a group of computers connected to share data or other resources.

data information that a computer processes or stores.

downloading transferring data from a server to a client computer's memory.

embedded computer a computer built into another device or object.

hardware the physical parts that make up computers and other electronics.

internet of things (IoT) the system of objects containing embedded computers that can send or receive data over the internet.

IP address a unique number that identifies each computer using the internet.

packet a piece of data transmitted through packet switching.

packet switching a way of sending data over the internet. In packet switching, the data is split into pieces, transmitted via different routes, then reconstructed at the destination.

server a computer that serves data to other computers in a network.

silicon a material used to make computer chips.

software computer programs.

uploading transferring data from a client computer's memory to a server.

URL (Uniform Resource Locator) the address of a website. A URL is also called a *web address.*

web browser a program that finds and displays web pages and other information from the internet.

web page a digital document that can be accessed using a web browser. A website is a collection of web pages.

World Wide Web the part of the internet that has websites.

GO ONLINE

Do you want to play a fun packet-switching game with your friends? Go to this website, and click on the Packet-Switching Game. You'll also find many other fun computer science games and activities!

www.worldbook.com/BuildingBlocks

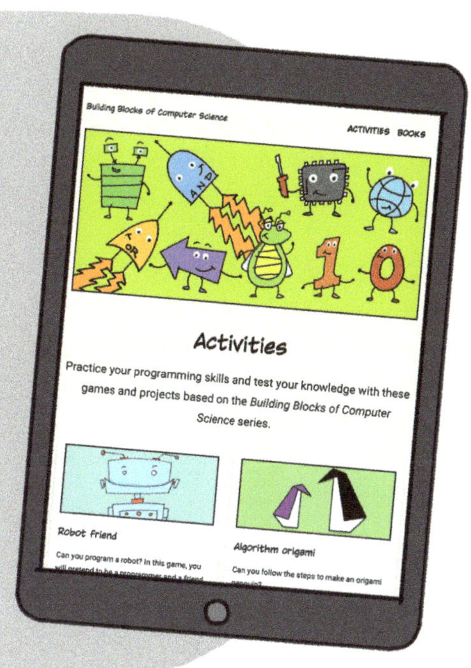

INDEX

www.ingramcontent.com/pod-product-compliance
Ingram Content Group UK Ltd.
Pitfield, Milton Keynes, MK11 3LW, UK
UKHW061958290726
14090UKWH00021B/1271